I0110844

Logan Merrick delivers an engaging chronicle of his experiences in the music business, and yet it's not really about the music business at all, but rather serves as a symbol of the things that can capture our hearts, and hold them hostage. He provides a thoughtful reminder of the looming presence of idols all around us, and the futility of chasing after those things that will ultimately leave us empty.

—Chad Segura-Meld Music

Logan's story strikes a power-chord for aspiring musicians and worship leaders. His style is easy to identify with and full of Scriptural wisdom. It's a clear call to humility and the real heart of worship that I truly needed to hear.

—Jerod McPherson,
National Youth Evangelist,
Christian Motorcyclists Association

"Sometimes the hardest thing to do is admit you have failed God. Idols aren't just physical objects, but anything that prohibits you from giving God your all. Chasing Dreams, Killing Idols gives the reader an inside look at the Christian music industry and how good intentions and dreams can quickly become idols in their own right. Author Logan Merrick's raw honesty and the way he deals with his struggles serve as an inspiration to anyone battling idols and offers an effective solution to get your walk with Christ back on track."

—Jay Heilman Founder &
Live Media Content Director
ChristianMusicReview.org &
KingdomBuilderTV

This book will be very helpful to provide some practical insight to the nature of idolatry and some real life applications to kill it. No matter where you might find yourself in life the truths in this book will help you take steps to remove yourself and your idols from the throne in your life and exalt Christ. This is a Gospel centered, Christ exalting read.

—**Logan McCourtney**
Student Pastor

Chasing Dreams, Killing Idols

A Story of Almost Famous

LOGAN MERRICK
&
TRACI MERRICK

LUCIDBOOKS

Chasing Dreams, Killing Idols

Copyrighted © 2014 by Logan Merrick

Published by Lucid Books in Houston, TX.
www.LucidBooks.net

All rights reserved. No part of this publication may be reproduced, stored in a retrieval system, or transmitted in any form by any means, electronic, mechanical, photocopy, recording, or otherwise, without the prior permission of the publisher, except as provided for by USA copyright law.

First Printing 2014

ISBN-13: 978-1-63296-016-0
ISBN-10: 1632960168

Special Sales: Most Lucid Books titles are available in special quantity discounts. Custom imprinting or excerpting can also be done to fit special needs. Contact Lucid Books at info@lucidbooks.net.

This book is dedicated to our sweet children,
Noah, Ariah, Eli and Micah.
May you four always be faithful to the call of Christ!

CONTENTS

ACKNOWLEDGMENTS

From Logan:

> I would like to thank the guys who find themselves in these pages. Thank you for our time together and the stories we share.

> Also a big thanks goes to those who gave to make this book possible:

> Sue Rowe, Rick and Susan Lochala, Betty and Burl Collingsworth, Samantha Secor, Angie and Leonard King, Kyle and Jenny Robertson, Charles and Sue Powell.

> Thank you all for your help and financial support to see this project through.

> To my loving wife who sat with me through the long hours of writing this—I can't express how much you mean to me. The patience you've had in the seasons of life we've shared has been astounding. You're my one true love whom I adore more than anything.

From Traci:

> Logan, you have been my partner in life for everything that matters—learning to be "grown ups," raising our beautiful children, leading ministries, and now writing this book. I hope you know that it has been my privilege to live this story with you and that I wouldn't change any part. Each difficult moment has been God's grace shaping us. Every good moment has been a gift that I've treasured. I'm so thankful for the godly man, husband and father that you are.

> I love you…always have and always will.

> Also thank you to my parents who have loved us unconditionally. I pray that we continue your legacy of love with our own children and their future spouses.

INTRODUCTION

T HIS IS A BOOK ABOUT my story. Throughout this book you will learn all about my shortcomings as a man and my sinful nature as a believer. I've failed much in my life and I fail a lot in this story. The one thing I don't say though in the chapters that follow are the things I did right. I don't want you to get the wrong impression of me. I'm not making a spectacle or trying to glorify my sin. I want this story to be one that is authentic and real, that lays it all out there and gets it all in the open. I feel that many of the problems in the church are that we're not authentic enough. We don't show the true us. We tend to gloss over and photoshop our lives together and put on a show for our church family and then leave never really getting to know each other. I want you to learn who I am, to understand that nothing about a stage, a book, or any other platform makes me different from you or anyone else. I'm a broken, sinful man in total need of God's beautiful grace and forgiveness and am blessed to be called his. Yes. This is a story of my failure, but it's ultimately a story of God's goodness and amazing grace.

The band did a lot of good. We tried hard to play many free dates to help smaller churches and ministries have a chance to have a good quality worship experience. We gave away much of our merchandise to fans who honestly didn't have the means to afford it. We would sleep on floors in homes, so as to get to really know our host church and it's people as well as cut down the cost of the event. We worked hard to be the "real deal" when it came to who we were. We were authentic while on stage. We never operated in a way that was put on or fake. If you ever saw us in person and worshipped with us, please know that what you experienced was five guys giving everything to the Lord, wanting to experience him and his presence in a new way with our new friends we were just meeting for the first time.

This is not a "tell all" story. If you bought this thinking there would be gossip or a drama filled reality show on paper, you have the wrong book. This is an honest story of me losing sight of the bigger picture and allowing my dream to become my demise.

Know that I'm so honored and humbled you would decide to take your hard earned money to purchase this book. There are many other titles and stories by some very amazing well known pastors and writers out there, and I'm amazed God would give me the chance to share with you right now, my heart. I pray this book would give you a new insight for chasing your dream. That it would bring about more clarity and focus. I pray that if you've got your priorities wrong, this book would help you to get them right. Know I'm praying for you because I want you to achieve that dream the Father placed in your heart the day you were born. I want you to not only achieve it, but I want you to do it in such a way that it brings CRAZY honor and glory to the one who gave it to you!

It's also my prayer that while reading these pages, every word constantly points straight to the creator and lover of our souls, Jesus Christ. Thank you again, let's get started!

CHAPTER ONE

"It is the normal state of the human heart to try to build its identity around something besides God."

—*Soren Kierkegaard*

I'LL NEVER FORGET THAT MOMENT. The car pulled into the parking lot and I caught a glimpse of my destiny in the large silver building before us. Built to emulate the Capitol in Washington D.C., I knew that the gleaming structure would live forever in my mind's eye. My stomach clenched into knots as I considered how long I had waited for this moment to arrive. For the first time in my life, I was going to be heard by a professional record label. Not only that, but I was about to enter their domain—setting foot inside the world where music was made. My dream was finally tangible.

Success was at my fingertips and I couldn't wait to reach out and touch it. My vision of the future was more clear than ever.

We walked in together, as the band of brothers we'd always claimed to be, and tried not to gawk as we approached the receptionist's desk. On the wall in front of us, televisions playing videos of top performing artists such as Needtobreathe, For

King and Country, and Group 1 Crew, filled the space. Their large flashing screens were a reminder to all who entered of the power held by the men behind these doors. As I daydreamed, I could see our band performing on those same screens in a year or two's time.

I snapped out of my daydream when our manager began to outline what key points our meeting with the leaders of the publishing department would cover. I made mental notes of everything he said until my attention was arrested by the ding of the elevator to our left. The doors opened and two men emerged, introducing themselves and inviting us to follow them. We made small talk as the elevator carried us to the publishing floor and the door opened to reveal yet another tantalizing glimpse into the future. Awestruck, I stared at countless gold and platinum albums lining the long corridor. Names of artists who I have admired and enjoyed over the years seemed to boast in the magic that can happen when the men in this place took an interest in your music. We were guided into a large corner office where we began a meeting that would set the tone for the following year. I didn't know it in that moment, but it was also a meeting that would set the stage for the unraveling of my band and my faith as a Christian"

But let me start from the beginning....

As a kid, when given a cassette tape or CD (yes, you read that right—I just said cassette tape), I would immediately look at the sleeve in the cover. That's pretty normal when you consider the awesome pictures, the lyrics, and even the dedications which are often included. What made my actions unique was the fact that I was not looking for those things—I was looking to see who produced it, who wrote the songs, and even who the artist and repertoire rep were. I continued this habit for the majority of my life, dreaming the day would come when I would have the chance to "rub shoulders" with and know the people behind the names I read. More importantly, I wanted for them to know me.

Every Saturday, my dad and I would go for a hair cut. As he drove, we'd listen to the radio and he would quiz me. "You know who's playing guitar there? You know what sparked the idea for this song?" were common questions directed toward me as the classic rock songs blared from the car speakers. I believe that it was in the front seat of that old Ford pickup that my love for music and desire to be a musician were birthed.

Now, let's fast forward a decade or two...

I'm a married twenty-something with kids of my own and I'm still dreaming of life as a musician. Willing to do whatever it takes to catch my "big break," I'm slowly destroying my marriage with impetuous decisions and foolhardy hopes. I've pulled stunts like walking out of work so that I could drive all night with my wife and infant son from Florida to North Carolina because I had a last minute chance to play in front of a gathering of record executives at a band competition. The winner would receive a record deal, and I was sure that this was my "big chance." Sadly, the result of that trip was a few harsh comments in the judges' feedback and a voicemail from my boss letting me know that I was fired. Looking back, I still wonder how my wife managed to stand by me no matter how crazy my choices made our life. There were many times when I made life even more difficult for us simply because I cared more about my dreams than our reality.

After that fateful trip, I finally decided to give up on being the next big thing. I'd had several experiences with the music industry that had left a bad taste in my mouth. At one encounter, a man who is a respected industry professional informed me that I would lose my zeal for Jesus as I matured and that "it would be a good thing." Comments like that encouraged me to finally let go and just walk away. At that point in my life, I also had a two year old son and one of my greatest fears was that he would grow up thinking that his dad was a failure. Hopping from job to job, trying to eke out a living between gigs, and praying to be able to pay rent wasn't the example I wanted to set for him. As a symbol of my decision to leave my dreams behind once and for all, I gave away my drum set. It was a custom kit that I had dreamed of having for years, but I knew that it was time to lay it on the altar in order to show God (and myself) that I was ready to move forward with my life. It was time to take care of my family the way I should have been from the beginning. No more wandering husband, no more unstable father who floats from one bad job to another as he dreams of greatness...it was time to be the man I needed to be. I took the first decent job I could find, enrolled in seminary, and started ministering part time as a youth pastor. My plan was to finish my degree and pursue full-time ministry. For the first time in a longer than I could remember, I was on a stable path and I felt good about it.

As time passed, I tried to maintain the peace that I had first felt when I made the decision to give up music. My wife and son were finally beginning to feel like life was stable and they seemed happy. I knew that I should be content, but secretly I continued to battle my inner longing for the band life. Deep within, I wanted to run hard one more time after that ever-elusive dream of playing the big stages. It felt good to know that I was finally making an honest living and providing for my family—something that I hadn't done for the entire length of my marriage—but that inner voice just couldn't be completely silenced. Then one day, for reasons only God knows, my dream landed back in my lap. I randomly met five other guys who were insanely talented musicians and who loved the Lord. We played together at a show that I had organized to help a local man with very serious medical issues. The funds raised would pay his medical debts and it was a cause that I was passionate about. The plan was to simply lead worship for the event and pray that God blessed the coffers for the sake of the cause.

At this point, most of us were working full-time jobs and some of us were on staff at local churches. Our focus was on our lives with no serious thoughts of traveling the nation and pursuing a music career. We played that night to support a good cause without any plan to continue once the music stopped.

We played three songs that night.

"You are the One," an original song written by our singer.

"Coming to Save Us," another original song that would later propel us into the Nashville Christian music scene.

And a cover of "How He Loves Us" by John Mark McMillan.

When we finished playing, the crowd went crazy. Fans in attendance said we should be a "real band". You know the drill—travel, lead worship and make a record. So that's what we did. That became the night that our band was born.

From the attention we received at that very first show in May 2010, we were booked almost every weekend for the rest of the year. Church camps, Sunday worship services, youth group events…we went from being non-existent to scrambling to meet the sudden demand for CDs and merchandise.

We recorded a two song CD sampler in Lakeland, Florida, which we began to give out for a donation. That sampler had the song "Coming to Save Us" on it which, as I already mentioned, would later open doors that we would have never thought possible.

So there we were—a fresh new band with their own CD, playing all over Central Florida—when our manager at the time gave me a call. He was a friend of mine who had been helping us book dates, and his call presented us with an opportunity that would help launch us forward. That was when my mind began to explode with the possibilities of what could be.

The band's early days!

CHAPTER TWO

*"Idolatry is worshipping anything that ought to be used,
or using anything that is meant to be worshipped."*

—*St. Augustine*

I DOLS. THEY'RE FUNNY THINGS. NOT funny "ha ha" of
course, but funny in the sense that, unless they're made
of gold and in the shape of a calf, you honestly don't even
notice their power over your time, focus, and energy. What
is an idol? Idols can be anything that we give our undivided
time, money, and affection to. Idols can literally be anything.
They can be as big as career aspirations or as small as social
media. They can be as harmful as a secret lover or as harmless
as our own children. Anything and everything can be an idol.
And everyone seems to have them at one point or another.
Why? Because everyone worships something. Created to be
in a worshipful relationship with the God of the universe, it
is instilled within us to be creatures of worship. Whether it's
ourselves, a self-made god, or the one true God, we were all
created to worship and that is what we will do in one capacity
or another. The problem we find with this worship habit is
that we often don't do what we were intended. Following
our fallen nature, we turn our worship from the One who

deserves it and lavish it upon the false idols we create. And what we need to know about false idols is this...they're dangerous.

It's easy to spot idols in the lives of others, but it seems that we're usually blind to them in our own. Unless we stop to take an earnest inventory of where our focus has been, or unless God intervenes and points out the things we've been putting in His place, we honestly don't even notice that we're bowing the knee at the altar of idols. They receive all the glory and relationship that the Father is due, and, in our telescopic view, we stay in oblivion.

In Exodus, we read all about a group of people who were desperate to find an object for their worship. The children of Israel, having just escaped the horrors of Egypt thanks to the One true God, were complaining to Aaron about their leader Moses' absence and their lack of a deity to worship. As the second-in-command, they apparently felt that it was Aaron's job to remedy these problems. So, in a response borne of panic (he feared the gathering mob), Aaron gathered their gold earrings and we see the story play out in Exodus 32:

> Exodus 32: 2-6 *"So Aaron said to them, "Take off the rings of gold that are in the ears of your wives, your sons, and your daughters, and bring them to me." So all the people took off the rings of gold that were in their ears and brought them to Aaron. And he received the gold from their hand and fashioned it with a graving tool and made a golden calf. And they said, "These are your gods, O Israel, who brought you up out of the land of Egypt!" When Aaron saw this, he built an altar before it.* **And Aaron made a proclamation and said, "Tomorrow shall be a feast to the Lord."** *6 And they rose up early the next day and offered burnt offerings and brought peace offerings. And the people sat down to eat and drink and rose up to play."* (ESV, emphasis mine)

You may or may not know the story of the golden calf really well, but what I hope you will see is why this ancient story is so very relevant for today,—it's something that repeats day after day in the hearts and lives of God's people even now. When you read it, you might do what I'm guilty of when reading a familiar text: skimming over it and missing some key points. That's why I emphasized the portion I did.

"And Aaron made a proclamation and said, "Tomorrow shall be a feast to the Lord."

Here's why it matters: Aaron ends up calling the idol "Lord!" He's creating a false god, the people are worshipping the gold which previously decorated their earlobes, and their hearts are far from Yahweh. BUT, to make it ok, they name the statue "Lord." That's similar to having an affair, but calling your lover by the name of your spouse. You aren't really cheating if you use the right name, right?

We are people who hate accountability. And so were the Israelites. We want what we want when we want it, but never want to be called on the carpet for our actions. When Aaron is confronted later in the story, we see him squirming to shift the blame from his own shoulders to that of anyone else he can think of.

Exodus 32:21-24 *"And Moses said to Aaron, "What did this people do to you that you have brought such a great sin upon them?" And Aaron said, "Let not the anger of my lord burn hot. You know the people, that they are set on evil. For they said to me, 'Make us gods who shall go before us. As for this Moses, the man who brought us up out of the land of Egypt, we do not know what has become of him.' So I said to them, 'Let any who have gold take it off.' So they gave it to me, and I threw it into the fire, and out came this calf."* (ESV)

Aaron begins by blaming the people...*"You know the people, that they are set on evil."*

Then he blames Moses...*"Moses, the man who brought us up out of the land of Egypt, we do not know what has become of him."*

Then he just starts grasping for straws in a desperate attempt to justify himself and take the heat off his own conscience...*"So they gave it to me, and I threw it into the fire, and out came this calf."*

I can just imagine Moses' face as Aaron talks.

He blames the people and sees that Moses isn't buying it. So Aaron switches tactics, "Hmmm.... well...Moses...they were all saying you didn't come back in a timely manner so, you know...I—I—I gotta keep everybody calm and collected before your handsome brother gets killed! "

Like a true brother would, Moses doesn't let him get away with it. "Whoa! What's that playa? You're blaming ME for this???"

So Aaron tries again, "you're right...you're so totally right! See what happened was...I took all the gold and just kind of threw it into the fire and out popped this fully formed, beautifully handcrafted, golden calf! Bro, you-should-have-seen-it, it was CRAZY!"

I don't know if you're like me or not, but when I read this I can't help but think that Israel is ridiculous. I mean, it's actually just amazing that God didn't strike Aaron dead right then and there. But let's talk about why I'm telling you this story and why I'm sharing about my own experiences.

You see, I'm not just telling you about my life because I think you would enjoy it (although I hope that you do). I'm telling you about it because I want you to see where I, and others like me, go so very wrong. Chasing my dreams ultimately took me down a path that turned out to be nothing more than the pursuit and worship of a golden calf. It turns out that I'm not so very different from those ridiculous Israelites...so I'd say

14

that it's a good thing that God wasn't into striking them dead or I wouldn't be alive to write these words today.

Let me be clear: I'm not saying that chasing your dream is like crafting a golden statue. I'm not even saying that chasing dreams is bad. In fact, I would never say that. I totally believe God places dreams inside us, and that He has a purpose for those dreams. Dreams are a great thing! But what I am saying is that dreams cannot control your life. When they do, you will find yourself bowing before some refurbished jewelry and then getting defensive when your idol comes to light.

And that's what this book is about.

My downfall was chasing a dream that turned into an idol.

Through these pages, we're going to talk about how to spot idols in your life and how to properly chase your dream without allowing it to control you. After that, we'll take a look at some of the things that people tend to put in the place of God most often and then address how the Bible deals with this issue. You see, we must first learn to recognize the idols in our lives before we can take steps to destroy them. As long as we're acting like Aaron—desperately grabbing for reasons to justify our sins—we'll remain in captivity. And when that happens, God is bound to intervene in one of two ways. First, because His love is too great to leave us in our mire, He'll do what it takes to uproot that idol. The bad thing about a God intervention like this is that it hurts a lot more to have something ripped from clenched fingers than to have it taken from an open palm. When God kills an idol that you aren't willing to kill yourself, it will hurt. Trust me, I know. The second option is that He will give you over to your pursuit of all that is not of Him and you'll find yourself in a tailspin of sin. Not pretty. I want you to understand, you and I were made to worship something greater than ourselves. Our creator, God, is much more worthy of our praise and affection and when we worship lesser things it cheapens our existence. We were created in His image and to worship Him and Him alone. Nothing else is worthy of that honor. If our lives aren't reflecting that truth, things will get ugly because we will soon find ourselves bound up in the junk that we've chosen to worship.

The Bible says our God is a jealous God. He is the only One who deserves our admiration and attention. He is the only One worthy of our worship. Nothing and no one should sit in His place. The Word also tells us that He is a good God. He created us to worship Him because it is good for us. By worshipping the Creator God, we walk in obedience and find worth and peace in our lives. But much like the Israelites, we want a god we can understand and control, a god of self-made existence. These gods will always let us down and bring about destruction and doom. You may already be feeling a tug on your conscience as you realize that there are things or people in your life who are currently sitting on His throne in your heart. That's a good thing! Like the writer of Hebrews says in chapter 12, *"Therefore, since we are surrounded by so great a cloud of witnesses, let us also lay aside every weight, and sin which clings so closely, and let us run with endurance the race that is set before us, looking to Jesus, the founder and perfecter of our faith..."* (**ESV**) (Emphasis mine).

The weight that you feel is the sin which we will deal with in the upcoming chapters.

Me at our FH table.

CHAPTER THREE

"Oh senseless man, who cannot possibly make a worm
or a flea and yet will create gods by the dozen!"

— *Michel de Montaigne*

NOW THAT WE'VE LAID SOME groundwork, let's continue with the story...the beginning of my dreams, the terrible crash back to earth, and the crisis of faith that ensued

After realizing we might be onto something bigger than we could have ever planned, like the crazy possibility of signing a major record contract, the guys and I were given the opportunity to play at the university we had all attended. One warm Florida evening, we led worship for a packed house of 1,000 passionate Jesus-following students. As we played praises to the Father, the music grew to a crescendo I will never forget. We were playing an original song and as the last chorus died out and the music faded away, we stood in amazement listening to the sound of 1000 voices singing the lines of our song. With worshipful abandon, the students proclaimed that the day when Jesus would redeem the world from sin, death, and pain was coming soon. Their voices rang out with conviction, confident of the victory we have in

Jesus, and my eyes filled with tears as I sensed the power of the Holy Spirit in that moment. These college kids sang out with everything in them, unrelenting in praise, and we band guys stood in awe. It was in that moment that we realized that we were no longer playing music. Somewhere in the midst of the melody, we had become witness to an amazing display of pure worship. And what's more? They were singing our song... pure, undulated adoration to the Father in the form of our lyrics, our chords, and the rhythm of my drums. They were singing our song and they were owning it— as they embraced the message behind them and the Savior who inspired them. We couldn't believe it. I remember realizing that this was the type of moment that bands and song writers can spend an entire career waiting to experience and I was humbled to see what God was doing. To this day, I have experienced few things that have overwhelmed me the way I was that night listening to those students sing the song which had been my own heart's cry long before those words were ever performed on a stage. Corey, the lead singer/songwriter and my friend, was blown away to hear the words the Holy Spirit had given him (which had been penned years ago on that very school campus!) now on the lips of the crowd who filled the chapel.

As this moment was taking place, our sound guy Josh was catching the entire thing on film. With his iPhone, he managed to film this amazing experience while the rest of us stood oblivious. After that night, we watched the video over and over as we relived the magic of that moment. It was later uploaded to YouTube for the world to see and became a turning point in our career. Remember when I said that our song would catch the attention of Nashville? Well...this was how. One night, one song, and a website called YouTube. A friend of ours managed to obtain the email address of a Grammy award-winning producer and promptly sent him a link to the video. From there, we were able to work with him to create our first five song CD (a replacement for the little two song sampler we'd been rolling around town with). After that, this same YouTube link found it's way into the hands of a man who manages several prominent Christian musicians, setting the stage for the day when he would become our manager. One seemingly insignificant song and one video shot with an iPhone opened doors for us that I could have never imagined or forced open on my own. The power of a true worship experience was what I believe had caught the attention of everyone who saw it.

From here, I will spare you a lot of boring details and simply hit on the "highlight" moments that occurred in the next year…

After signing with our new manager, we proceeded to secure a booking contract with a large agency in the Nashville area. Things began to progress rapidly as we attended meeting after meeting with one high profile label after another. We focused a great deal of time and attention on trying to discern who would be the best partner for us and who would understand our vision for ministry. We also were blessed to partner with a missions-oriented ministry called Food for the Hungry and we found a lot of joy in being able to play a role in helping families around the world. Through the sponsorships we promoted, children and families in third world countries were able to receive food and medical care that would otherwise be unavailable to them. Having this "missions" branch of our ministry meant a lot to us because it was our heart to impact the world in more ways than just music.

After FFH came on board, we began meeting with our manager on a monthly basis as we planned tours, played dates, wrote songs, and participated in various photo and video shoots. Thanks to this, I can now say that I know the drive from Florida to Nashville like the back of my hand. Every exit, pothole, fast food restaurant, and clean (or dirty) bathroom became a sort of second home thanks to the hours I spent on the road. Six months in, it's easy to see how all the moving and meetings could begin to take its toll. My bandmates and I were all feeling the pressure of wondering when we would finally "make it." As bills piled up, money became more of an issue as we struggled to find a way to make enough to support ourselves. As fast as things were progressing, it still wasn't fast enough to keep up with the monthly expenses of five guys (three of us were married and I also had two kids!). It didn't seem to matter how many dates we were able to play, after every one of our partners received their share and the expenses were paid, there just wasn't anything left. It was with this stress of finances looming over us that we began to feel more and more impatient with the pace things were progressing at.

Meetings came and went. We'd walk into the offices of major labels, play our music, answer questions, and then walk right back out. There never seemed to be a moment when we truly knew where we stood. There was a continual sense of "fake" that seemed to overshadow Nashville, and we struggled to find our way without compromising our heart to be an authentic worship band. Ironically, Nashville was having an affect on us no matter what we said. As more dates were played and more meetings took place, we began to feel that we were owed recognition, money and especially fame.

Days on the road grew longer as well until the sweet sense of unity and mission we'd felt at the beginning became a distant memory. It was no longer about the passion of seeing people's lives changed through an experience with Jesus. Now it was real! There were people depending on us to make this happen and it was our job to see it through. The idea that we had to focus day and night or we'd be failures became the unspoken message tattooed on our subconscious minds. No matter how much time we spent praying and fasting together, the pressure was relentless and we dared not speak of it. Of course, we could all feel it—the pressure to perform, the frustration with our bandmates, aggravation over our financial situations and the seeming lack of definite progress. It was festering, getting ready to burst like a geyser. Under the surface, it lurked...until the night the dam broke. And it was devastating.

We had just finished playing a conference in various parts of the Northeast and were now making the long drive to Ohio for yet another conference. We were all exhausted as we rolled into town. I'd had a great idea to help us make some extra cash by performing a live concert via the internet and selling tickets online. The guys were hungry and ready to call it a day, but with a little persuasion by me, they agreed to do it. After dinner, we set up the camera and sound equipment and posted the event on Facebook and Twitter to let our fans know that we'd be playing live and taking requests. As Josh tweaked the last few knobs for our sound, the seconds were ticking down for the show to begin. Within fifteen minutes, our live stream had completely sold out. Our fans were obviously excited about this impromptu special session. Personally, I was really excited that my idea had worked and would help put some more funds in the coffers! As "go time" drew near, I noticed that the singer, Corey, was acting distant. I asked him what was wrong and he downplayed it by saying that he was tired. Not believing him, I pressed for a more genuine answer until he admitted that he felt like I'd pressured him into doing this show. He was tired and not interested in performing that night when all he really wanted was to relax before the conference taking place the next morning.

I don't always do well with people who question or accuse me. Like most people, I get defensive. It wasn't that Corey was necessarily being mean. Looking back, I can see his perspective with a lot more compassion than I did that night. But on that particular night, when I was tired and really feeling the pressure of being the only band guy with a wife and kids depending on me, the "redeemed" version of Logan did not shine through. Without adequate God time and frustrated by his lack of appreciation for my *obviously* brilliant idea, "Christian Logan" died a quick death, and fallen nature, sinful, potty-mouth Logan came out with a roar!

When Corey said that he wouldn't do the show, I said some things that I'm not proud of. I would even confess that I said things that no one should say to an enemy...let alone a friend. I yelled at the top of my lungs, cussing him, while the other band guys sat in stunned silence.

Have you ever done something like this? Have you ever just torn someone down through your words? It's crazy, right? It's like you have no idea where these feelings and words are coming from but they're just pouring from you like hot water from a faucet. I know now that it was coming from a heart of pride. Issues that I had held in and frustrations that were haunting me came out in a cowardice flood of yelling rather than a rational discussion with the goal of reconciliation. I felt so justified! We needed the money, our fans loved this private show, and it needed to happen. Of course, the greater truth was that I hated the fact that he wasn't abiding by my rules.

After all was said and done, I stormed out and went to my room. In there, I broke down and cried, knowing in my heart that I'd crossed a line that I could never undo. I knew that, no matter how well I apologized, things would be different from this moment on and the band would be forever changed. This was the beginning of the end for me and for Letters From Patmos.

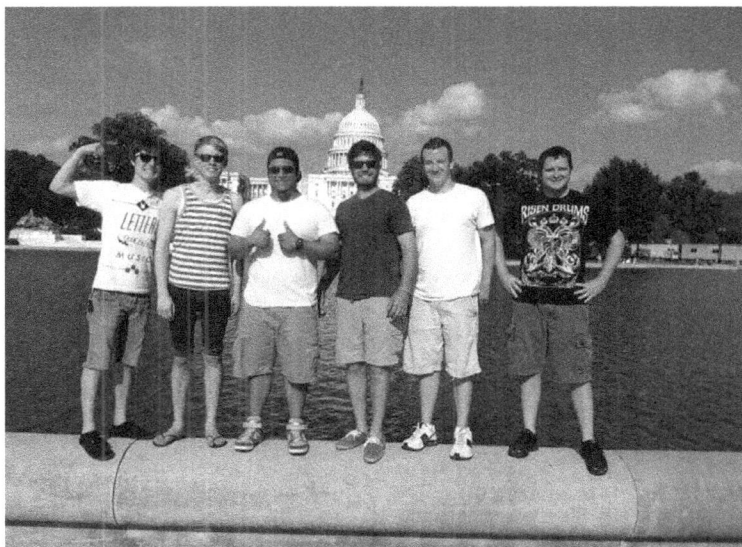

Walking around Washington, DC on our off day.

CHAPTER FOUR

"Idolatry is when you become the source of your own joy. Poverty of spirit is a wonderful thing."

— *Paul Washer*

For freedom Christ has set us free; stand firm therefore, and do not submit again to a yoke of slavery.

—Galations 5:1

READ THIS VERSE. THEN READ it again. Get really familiar with it because we are about to break it apart and take a close look at what Paul is saying to us through this text.

"For freedom Christ has set us free."

Awesome! Wait...what? What do we need freedom from? Sin? Sounds right. So Christ came to give us eternal life and to set the captives free from sin. Note that he's not saying that you won't sin any longer, but that sin's power has been broken.

"Stand firm therefore..."

Stand firm in the freedom that came when sin's power was broken. It came at a cost.

"And do not submit again to the yoke of slavery."

Idols bring slavery!

As we make our way through the rest of this chapter and book we're going to see that idols are sin. It's sin because it's worshiping something other than the one true God who deserves all our affection and adoration. And what does sin do? It enslaves us. So this is where I'm going to camp out for the rest of the chapter and a few to come. I want to dive more deeply into what I call the "symptoms" of idolatry and the effect that they have on the lives of those they enslave. It's just like a doctor's examination in which they look at your symptoms in order to diagnose an illness. We will do the same thing with idolatry as we take a peek into your life. I battled these symptoms and have felt the effects of their pull, so I know them well and my prayer is that this book will help you ensure that any battle you may face with the idols in your life ends in victory. But it all starts with the right diagnosis.

The first symptom and probably the earliest one to detect is obsession.

If you will recall the first chapter, you'll see that I talked about how, even from childhood, I was totally obsessed with the music industry, who was in it and all of that. But in my childhood, it was an innocent hobby. As I grew older and developed who I was as a musician, it became a true obsession.

When the band started to take off, my obsessive ways began to kick in like a second nature. It's totally crazy for me to think back to those days now, realizing that every waking moment I was thinking about, talking about, and researching the band, our career and where it was going. Literally, as soon as I woke up in the morning, my first thought was always "what can I do to help push the band forward?" And please note that I use the term "push" because this endeavor had already ventured out of God-driven territory and into the realm of my own efforts. Because I was the one that dealt with the business side of things such as booking, thinking of new ways to promote our product and gaining more exposure for us, it was easy for me to take ownership of steering the band. How could we build our brand? Or the way our manager would put it, "how to build our pizza shop and have the best pizza in town?" That's what drove me. That's what made my engine stay rev'd high all the time. The band, our image, fame, and vision for ministry consumed my every waking hour and thought. I couldn't leave it alone.

It was so hard for me to turn off the part of my brain that wanted to continually think about the band, money and fame, that when I would come home from being gone on tour my wife would say things like, "Logan, could you be present with us? Would you make a better effort to be with me and the kids?" We would argue because I was always on my phone or on the internet trying to get more dates for our upcoming tours. I drove our manager crazy because I would repeatedly call him wanting to know what the record execs were saying about our songs. He would always tell me that I had to quit calling so much and that I was becoming a nuisance. I always justified my obsessive ways by saying "Hey! This is my business. I want to be successful and provide well for my family while doing what I love." It sounded good to me, even if they weren't buying it. *I'm not only doing this because I love it, but because it's what's going to be best for my family in the end. Sure, they're paying the price now because I'm always gone. Yes, I'm distracted during the rare times I'm home because I have to focus all my attention on the band. But it will pay off one day soon and they'll be thankful for my drive and all the hard work I'm doing!*

Let me pause here and ask—are you justifying your sin? Do you find yourself sacrificing your family on the altar of idolatry? I promise you this, the one true God that should be receiving the focus would NEVER ask you to sacrifice your family for your dream. He created family. He loves family and healthy relationships. Your relationship with your wife and children comes directly after your relationship with your Savior. I want you to put the book down right now and ask yourself honestly—do I have my priorities in order? Is it God first, and my family second? Now, ask your spouse (if you aren't married, ask a roommate or close friend) if you've been way too obsessive lately. If either of you can say that you don't have your priorities in order than we have a problem and we've got to fix it immediately!

I won't even pretend that I don't have an obsessive personality...because I do. My wife and close friends can vouch that if I get excited about something or am passionate about accomplishing a goal, I'm like a dog with a bone. Sometimes this can be a good thing. Most of the time, it's not.

I'll be completely honest and admit that even writing this book has required a great deal of discipline in my thought life and down time. I've worked to hold myself accountable and have asked my wife to hold me accountable by telling me when I'm becoming obsessed. How ironic would it be to make a book about idolatry the idol of your life? I want to share that my heart for this book is not fame or fortune. I'm writing it because l have experienced what it means to fail at balancing my faith, family and dreams, and one of my greatest desires is to help you make better life choices than I did. I know, without even knowing you, how loved you are by God and I don't want idolatry to hinder you from experiencing the amazing plans He has for your life.

So how do we keep from obsessing? Well Paul gives us the answer in Colossians 3:2,

> **"Set your minds on things that are above, not on things that are on earth."**

Paul is telling us to think about Heaven, the eternal, Christ and His glory...the things that matter. This doesn't happen effortlessly. We must discipline ourselves everyday to focus on Christ's kingdom and His righteousness and goodness. *"Set your mind on the things above"* by disciplining yourself to open your eyes each morning with a plan to be intentional in fellowshipping with your Heavenly Father. What better way to set the tone of your day than by preparing your spirit with a time of prayer and thanksgiving?

What happens if you do the opposite, as Paul puts it, and set your mind on "things of the earth?" If we keep reading Colossians 3 we find out:

> **Put to death therefore what is earthly in you: sexual immorality, impurity, passion, evil desire, and covetousness, which is idolatry.**

What's inside of you, that which is "earthly," includes "sexual immorality, impurity, and covetousness which is idolatry." Those things begin to take you down paths you never intended.

Let me give you some examples.

We have pastors who have been caught committing adultery, addicted to pornography, and so forth. I don't believe for one second that these pastors ever intended on being cheating, porn-addicted husbands and fathers. I'm sure they started out like anyone else. They felt the call to pastoring, loved the Lord, fellowshipped with Him, and enjoyed teaching His word to people. So what happened? They began to develop small chinks in their armor. They got sidetracked. They quit setting their minds on the things above and became consumed by ministry, people, business, and "life." It's probably easy to imagine that some could have been obsessed with building their own kingdom. As they slowly but surely took their eyes off of the Father and placed the focus on themselves, their idols gave the forces of darkness power over them. And by power I mean the ability to distract them and unconscious permission to redirect their God-given dreams into self-driven nightmares. If the enemy can distract you by keeping you busy and out of communion with God, then he's got you. Pretty soon, other sins begin to crop up until you have begun the precarious slide down a path that leads to compromised integrity and a ruined reputation. Remember Paul's warning—sin is slavery. Once we open the door, we are sure to find ourselves ensnared.

When seeking and chasing a dream, you must learn to walk within the very fine balance of chasing and being consistent without being obsessive. This will be easier for some than others. For those who are extremely goal-oriented and driven, the entrepreneur types, this will be extremely difficult. I'm a natural-born entrepreneur, so if you share that make up, let me be the first to tell you that you need accountability. Gather a group of people who believe in your dream, who understand your vision and what God has called you to, but who will also hold you accountable for your actions and will call you out when you're pushing too hard or becoming unbalanced. They will have to be bold people to do this because it is not easy. And you must be willing to listen and not react angrily. You have to trust that if these people are seeing it, than it's likely that you're out of balance and probably need to put your dream on hold for a bit and slow down.

For those who do not share my personality type, I would still encourage you to take a hard look at your own tendencies. While you may not share my determination to "make" a dream happen, you may find that your personality lends itself to bitterness as you watch others pursue their dreams and take risks that you could not find the courage to take. Or perhaps you have come to view your dream as a means of escape? Confident that, if you can just achieve it, you will be happy, you've placed your dream in the role of savior of your life. Whatever your tendency, it is easy for every one of us to find ourselves out of balance as we pursue the dream God has placed within us.

Regardless of your personality type, there are a few things that can help us all to maintain the delicate balance we need to be godly dream chasers. As we wrap up this chapter let me give you a quick recap in the form of a "to do" list:

1. Obtain a small accountability group.

2. Journal everyday about your journey.

3. Have a daily Bible reading schedule.

4. Before you do anything, while you are still laying in bed each morning, take time to thank God for what He's doing in your life and to just enjoy being with Him. If need be, begin with just five minutes and work your way up. Just make sure that you set your alarm accordingly.

If you would commit to doing these four small things, I can guarantee that your battle with idolatry will lose some of its strength. When we are determined to keep our focus where it belongs (on Jesus), we are able to walk in balance in even the most tempting areas of our lives. These points will help keep you focused and balanced as you chase what God has called you to to.

Bus Time!

CHAPTER FIVE

*No matter how dear you are to God, if pride is harbored
in your spirit, He will whip it out of you. They that go
up in their own estimation must come down again by
His discipline.*

—*Charles Spurgeon*

*Spiritual pride is the illusion that you are competent to
run your own life, achieve your own sense of self worth,
and find a purpose big enough to give you meaning in
life without God.*

—*Tim Keller*

WHAT IF I TOLD YOU that God would make you
famous? That you could be the most powerful man
or woman in all the world? What if I offered you
wealth that would make Bill Gates seem like a pauper? And
all you have to do to attain all of these things is to listen to a
man who will be God's mouthpiece in your life and will give
you godly counsel and guidance! You also have to seek God
each day, every day, for your entire life, but that's easy because

you'll have this man to help you and you'll be living in ease and prosperity. Sounds good, huh? If I told you that, you'd probably accuse me of being a prosperity preacher...looking to fleece the flock with my own message of holy wealth. You'd likely start scanning the pages of this book in search of a request to send me a $50 check in order to gain your blessing of riches through my anointing. But, you'd be wrong.

Biblically, such a man did exist. He had wealth, military power, fame and all the things that come with the life of a celebrity. In other words, he was on the cover of "Hebrew Weekly" every single week! He was the talk of the town—the man every young boy longed to be and every young girl longed to marry. He was THAT guy! And the only thing he had to do to maintain his status was to listen to his godly counsel and to seek the face of God daily. Sounds like a good deal, right? So who was he? Well, I'll tell you his story. His name was Uzziah and we can read all about him in 2 Chronicles 26. Starting in verse 8, we read...

> "He set himself to seek God in the days of Zechariah, who instructed him in the fear of God, and as long as he sought the Lord, God made him prosper." (ESV)

And there you have it! No prosperity message from me, just something straight from the Scripture. But before I go any further into that, I want to note something that is of utmost importance. The text states that Zechariah "instructed him in the fear of God." You'll need to remember this as the chapter continues because we will soon find that Uzziah succumbs to what is in the heart of any who don't properly grasp the fear of God. Which leads us to the question—what is the fear of the Lord? What does that even mean? We read passages throughout scripture that say,

> *"The fear of the Lord is the beginning of knowledge"*
> —Proverbs 1:7 (ESV)

Chapter Five

"And he said to man 'Behold, the fear of the Lord, that is wisdom and to turn away from evil is understanding".

—Job 28:28 (ESV)

Then a great one that, to me, really sums up what the fear of the Lord is about...

"Let all the earth fear the Lord; let all the inhabitants of the world stand in awe of him!"

—Psalm 33:8 (ESV)

So what is it? Simply put, the fear of God is being in awe of Him. Think about it...we are talking about the CREATOR OF THE UNIVERSE. He stands outside of time! He's the beginning and the end. He knows the thoughts of my innermost being and knows the number of hairs on my head. Why wouldn't we be in awe of Him? We stand in awe of guys that are seven feet tall and can dunk a basketball, for crying out loud! We stand in awe of guys who can bench press me and my whole family. And yet the God who created each of these uniquely talented men is usually overlooked and under-feared. Now, you may be saying, "I fear God!" But I would challenge you to truly evaluate your heart as to whether or not you actually do. A good self-check can be found by asking yourself, "Do I continue to sin in the same areas despite my promises and best intentions to stop?" If we truly grasped the magnitude and holiness of God, I believe that we'd all walk and talk a lot differently.

To fear God is to stand in awe of Him and His majesty. It's also, as Job tells us, to listen to His counsel and heed His warnings to run from evil. This means that we become people who are passionate about ridding our lives of the sin that would tangle us up and keep us from drawing closer to the One we admire—God.

CHASING DREAMS, KILLING IDOLS

The next symptom of this disgusting disease known as idolatry is not just a symptom—it's a rotting disease all on it's own which found its way into heaven long before we experienced it here on earth. It all started with a name I'm sure you've heard—Lucifer (aka Satan). He was an angel who thought he could do a better job at running things. Specifically, he said this:

'I will ascend to heaven; above the stars of God I will set my throne on high; I will sit on the mount of assembly in the far reaches of the north; I will ascend above the heights of the clouds; I will make myself like the Most High."

—Isaiah 14:13-15.

So what symptom am I referring to? You might have already guessed it—pride. Pride is at the very core of sin and it's what motivated Satan so long ago. It comes about in the moments when we begin to think that we "know better" than God. When we look at our own interests, wants and desires and decide that God's way is not trustworthy, valuable, or even validated, we are walking in the sin of pride. It consumes Satan and will easily overtake us if we are not vigilant. What makes it the most tricky is that it is so easy to spot in others, but so very hard to see in ourselves! Everyone hates that celebrity or random person who is consumed with self-promotion and pride. We love to hear stories about people who are humbled after spending their time looking down on those around them. What we find difficult is realizing that this ugly trait is often evident in our own lives while we remain blithely unaware. In *Mere Christianity*, C.S. Lewis says "pride is the one vice of which no man in the world is free; which every one in the world loathes when he sees it in someone else..."

Pride is a poison, or as Lewis puts it a *"vice,"* that leads us to other sins and vices. It's the "gateway drug" of sin, if you will. Think I'm exaggerating? Tell me the first sin that was ever committed. Way back when, in the Garden of Eden where Adam and Eve happily strolled the plush earth, what caused them to break our world and separate our spirits from harmony with the Creator? Wanting to eat some fruit? No. It was their desire to be like God and their failure to fear Him. And what is at the root of that? Pride! The first sin in history. With that in mind, I think we can agree that no one is absent from the struggle in this area.

Here in the Western part of the world, we are constantly comparing ourselves to others. Who is the slimmest? The smartest? The richest? The most witty? It's what motivates us to continue to strive to be better, have bigger, and elevate higher. You can see it in the Facebook photo albums featuring new cars, extravagant vacations, and "easy money" lifestyles. Pride says "I deserve this." And, ironically, it leads us to believe that its pursuit will bring us along the path of a good life. It disguises its ugliness through the promise of something better than what we feel we have. For Adam and Eve, it was the knowledge of God. For those of us chasing dreams, it may be the ability to achieve success and receive the acclaim or wealth we've always desired. But one thing is certain—no matter how promising it may seem, pride always brings death. Meanwhile, the Savior of the universe beckons us to walk in lowliness and humility, forsaking the glitter of this world and becoming the least of these as He promises real life. To put that in the context of pursuing our dreams, pride will always bring about the destruction that the Scriptures forewarn us about. Meanwhile, a dream pursued in humility and faith will lead to God being honored and our lives evidencing His peace and hope. Because our Heavenly Father wants good things for His children, He hates pride and the consequences that it brings about. The Bible repeatedly reminds us to live humbly and allow the Lord to exalt us according to His will.

So now that we've tacked down the role of pride in our

lives, let's go back to our boy Uzziah and see what becomes of the world's most powerful man when we pick up the story in verse 16:

"But when he was strong, he grew proud, to his destruction."

Uzziah was given everything. As long as he leaned heavily upon the Lord and remembered that he couldn't make it without God and His grace, Uzziah would continue to enjoy a place of greatness. We see in this verse that the author notes, "he was strong." And that became his downfall. Mistakenly believing that his military prowess, his fame and fortune were all the result of his own genius and power, Uzziah failed to walk in the fear of God. The result? He became a leper and died alone in a pretty inglorious end to such an illustrious life.

I can identify with Uzziah on a small scale. No, I've never had even a fraction of the wealth or fame or power that he enjoyed. And no, I'm not in danger of dying a leper. But I did mistake the hand of God on my life for my own wisdom and accomplishment. You see, as time went by and the band's popularity grew, I began to credit myself for the hard work I'd put into bringing us so far. When labels knew my name and people in churches across the nation were singing our songs, I'd give myself a small pat on the back in recognition of the kingdom I was building. I knew it was only a matter of time before the whole world knew my name and Letters From Patmos. And it was there, in those moments, where I met my destruction. The moment that I lost my fear of God—my awe of all He was doing and had done—was the moment the Lord brought me low. But I'll tell you the end of that story in the following chapter. First, I want to talk about how to avoid my mistake. How do we combat pride?

Through His beautiful, selfless life, Jesus shows us that

pride can only be defeated through humility. In a memorable display of true servanthood, Jesus completes His time on earth by washing the feet of his disciples before He journeys to the cross. Think about that a moment. In a time when the automobiles they were driving had four legs and some pretty foul "exhaust," these were the feet of men who had walked streets of manure! And, not only does Jesus wash their feet knowing how rank they must have been, but also knowing that some of these same men would grossly wrong him. Judas the betrayer...Peter the denier...Thomas the doubter...these weren't men who would never fail. Which begs the question, what would you do? Would you serve someone who would betray you? Someone who gossips about you and spreads lies throughout the community about your integrity or your morality? Someone who even finds satisfaction in seeing you hurt or ostracized? Personally, I wouldn't get them a cold drink on a hot day! And yet here we find the Savior of the universe kneeling in servitude to wash the feet of these unworthy men. THAT is a life marked by humility. And THAT is the means Christ gives us to show the world that we are different. Until the day He returns, He has called us to combat pride through a life of service and to live out the truth that we are set apart by a love without limits. Paul says this in Philippians 2:3-8

"Do nothing from selfish ambition or conceit, but in humility count others more significant than yourselves. Let each of you look not only to his own interests, but also to the interests of others. Have this mind among yourselves, which is yours in Christ Jesus, who though he was in the form of God, did not count equality with God something to be grasped, but emptied himself by taking the form of a servant, being born in the likeness of men. And being found in human form, he humbled himself by becoming obedient to the point of death, even death on a cross."

So, do you want to combat the pride in your life? Do you want to grow in humility? Don't start by willing yourself to be more humble! Why? Because this is still self-focused, which is the opposite of true humility. In order to cultivate a spirit of humility you must begin by learning to take the focus off yourself and to only concern yourself with those around you. And how does that relate to achieving your dreams?

If you want to live your dream, you must help someone else achieve their dream first.

CHAPTER SIX

The jealous are troublesome to others, but a torment to themselves.

—William Penn, *Some Fruits of Solitude, 1693*

THE THIRD AND FINAL "SYMPTOM" of idolatry is one that can be sneaky. It's similar to pride, and we all battle it in some way or another. What is it? Envy. Otherwise known as jealousy, envy is tough to diagnose because we can envy someone or be jealous of others without ever realizing that the ones we're jealous of, aren't at the root of our issue. So who or what is? If it's not the guy next door who just bought a new boat, then who is to blame? The answer is GOD!

Right now you might be thinking to yourself, *"No way! I don't blame God for my jealousy of _____."* And that, friend, is why it's so tricky! Before I delve into the reasons that God is at the center of our envy issues, let me tell you a little about how I struggled with jealousy in the band.

Many people think that most band stories begin with a moment of "overnight success." As members of the crowd, we tend to buy into the fairytale that anyone appearing on the stage must have hit it big overnight. At least, that's what I always thought. To the consumer, success does seem that way. Yesterday, no one had heard of this person or band and now they're all over the radio, television, internet or whatever. Surely they just began their pursuit of fame a couple weeks ago, right? Wrong! What the consumer can't see is the years of hard work and sacrifice that led up to this moment on stage and the appearance of "instant" celebrity. I'm not saying that there aren't rare cases when someone is able to arrive without paying the price. That can happen. But you'll notice that those cases don't tend to have to longstanding success. This is a truth that proves itself in any scenario—not just the entertainment industry. Take a look at your place of work. Someone who has not earned the position they hold will likely disappear as quickly as they appeared. Look at the musicians and performers that have exploded quickly, claimed their 15 minutes of fame, and then vanished. This is because you can't sustain something that you never learned to work for to begin with. Without earning your stripes it can be tough, if not impossible, to have the mental and emotional fortitude required to maintain the platform you've gained. So why am I telling you all of this?

Because I struggled with this in the band. As we were in negotiations with labels, I would call our manager completely irate because some band I'd never heard of had just announced a major record deal. These conversations always ended the same way—with me yelling at our manager that our deal was taking too long. He would then remind me that everything in life is a process and that I'd have to be patient. The label and our fans deserved to see how hard we were willing to work for recognition. I always hated that rebuttal. After hanging up, I would burn so badly with jealousy that I couldn't stand still. Envious over someone else's success and frustrated with our continued delay, I'd find fault with every song that band released on their debut album. Talking about how stupid it was that this band would be signed while we continued on hold, I'd secretly wish that they would fail and prove to be a waste for the label. Awesome, aren't I? What kind of brother in Christ and fellow musician wishes ill on someone like that? A jealous one—that's who! Jealousy makes us do or think crazy stuff.

Probably the most famous biblical story of jealousy is found with the "king" of crazy—King Saul. If you're not familiar with him, I'll hit the highlights of his story and let you read the whole sordid tale for yourself in the book of 1 Samuel. Saul was the king of Israel, anointed by God because the people had asked for a ruler. Unfortunately, he was a pretty sorry excuse for royalty. Not only was he a coward, he was also very prideful. I think we can safely say that if he lived today, his favorite pastime would be reading his own headlines. Similar to Uzziah, God had appointed a prophet named Samuel to help guide Saul. All he had to do was listen to Samuel's godly counsel and things would go well. Also similar to Uzziah, Saul grew arrogant and allowed pride to gain control of his heart, leaving him vulnerable to making some pretty poor choices. So let's fast forward a little and look into what's going on behind the scenes during Saul's rule.

Unbeknownst to Saul, God has Samuel anoint David as the future king of Israel while he is a young boy. David was a young boy with a heart for God. In fact, the Bible tells us that God Himself declared David to have a "heart like His." David understood that he could do nothing apart from God and he was completely confident in the Lord. He knew that his own abilities could never measure up to the might of God and that is what made him Israel's greatest king. As time goes by, others are drawn to the purity of heart that resides in David and he begins to gain a following. As you can imagine, this doesn't sit well with Saul. One day after a hard battle, something happens that pushes an ever-increasingly jealous Saul over the edge. The army is making its way through the streets and the women of the city are singing their victory praises. The tune they've chosen is catchy and Saul finds himself humming along...until the lyrics catch his ear.

"Saul has struck down his thousands, and David his ten thousands."

Ever heard of the straw that broke the camel's back? Oh snap! Saul goes crazy! From this moment on, Saul develops this nasty habit of pitching spears David's direction anytime the poor kid is nearby. David is no longer a noble young man to be discipled. He has become a rival in Saul's eyes. Saul can no longer see David's loyalty (which he maintained despite Saul's craziness!) because he is blinded by his jealousy. In contrast, David continues to remain true to Saul—no matter how many murder attempts the king makes. David even finds himself with an opportunity to get even by killing Saul. Having been run out of the city and forced to live in the mountains, David finds Saul unarmed and unaware in a cave. It would have been the perfect moment to bring all his problems to an end, but David resists the urge to kill Saul. He understood that God had chosen Saul as the leader of the people of Israel and that his end was not to come by David's hand. Sadly, Saul never realizes this same truth about the omnipotence of God and the perfection found in His timing. He continues to pursue David, driven by insecurity and jealousy, until the day comes when he chooses suicide. Seeing that the army of the Philistines were gaining victory over him in battle, Saul succumbs to pride one last time and chooses to fall on his sword rather than face defeat. His death is a final symbol of how opposite David and Saul truly are.

Saul, consumed with pride and obsessed with his self-image, succumbs to jealousy of a young boy (who, for the record, didn't seem to have any intention of trying to steal Saul's throne). The moment he gave himself over to this jealousy, his fate was sealed. Unable to do a quality job as the ruler and protector of his people, Saul authors his own end through a suicide. All this because he was so crazy with jealousy that he was unable to be the man God had called him to be. Lacking a solid foundation in God's sovereignty and love, the king became distracted by his insecurities and gave credence to the idea that everyone was out to get him. It caused him to cling to the very thing God had given him (his kingship), to fear anyone he perceived to be a threat (David), and to ultimately lose everything he sought to control. Sound familiar?

David, on the other hand, had a foundational understanding that God was (and still is!) sovereign and in control of every aspect of life. Although the waiting process was difficult, he understood that life is a process and chose to trust God to fulfill His promise.

Jealousy can make you think and do silly things. Just as I talked about the crazy things Saul was doing because of jealousy, I too found myself doing crazy things. And it has been jealousy in my own life that has made me think ridiculous things and act out accordingly. In the band, this time came when I found myself jealous of my band mates. Crazy, right? I mean, we're all in the same group! Who gets jealous of guys in the same beat as you? They were struggling financially, just like me. They were waiting for this seemingly unending process, just like me. They were traveling and working just as hard as I was to make this dream a reality. What in the world would I be jealous of? The honest answer is that I was jealous of their gifting. Feeling threatened by how talented the other guys in the band were, I would go into moments of internal panic attacks where crazy thoughts would take over. I'd start to fear that they were planning to kick me out of the band and find a better drummer (which they weren't). I'd imagine that they were thinking of all the ways I was holding them back musically (which I wasn't). Even worse, I believed that they viewed me as the weak link because I was the one with a family (a wife and 2 kids). In those moments, I felt sure that they'd be relieved to find someone who was single and would free them to do whatever they wanted without worrying about responsibilities. The truth was that these thoughts never crossed their minds. They weren't scheming or begrudging me for my children or inadequacies. In fact, they loved my wife and kids and felt like I was a talented drummer.

Envy makes us into conspiracy theorists that are looking for a way to validate our craziness. It causes us to act ridiculously because, at the root of the problem, it encourages us to believe the lie that God is not trustworthy. Envy tempts us to believe that we can't trust God because He isn't really good—He didn't give us the right giftings or enough talent and He's not ordering our lives according to the plans we've made or the expectations we have. Without this basic belief that God is good, we aren't able to trust that He has our ultimate best interest in mind. We become blinded by the view of others succeeding and, in bitterness, we curse Him for failing to bring the same blessing about in our own lives rather than cursing them for being blessed. Why? Because we know that they aren't to blame. And there is the heart of the matter. God is at the center of our jealousy because, ultimately, our envy is based on our perception of Him rather than on the success of those around us. Of course, most who call themselves Christians struggle to openly admit this truth, but it remains true just the same. We blame God. We envy and covet other's lives, blessings, and giftings. We ask why they are blessed, outlining the reasons they don't deserve those good things. *They don't go to church nearly as often as I do. Are they even Christians? They're lazy—they don't even use that gift to its full advantage.* And we complain to God that He has chosen to show them His goodness while we remain on the sidelines sucking eggs.

Personally, I wasn't trusting God. I can say that in complete honesty. I had put all my trust in our manager, the label we were hoping to sign with, the talent of the band, and my own ability to work hard and promote us. Along the way, I had forgotten that this was about God. Clutching the gift He'd freely given me—the opportunity to be part of a pure worship experience—I mirrored King Saul as I began to suspect that God couldn't be trusted. When I saw others getting blessed, I'd angrily exclaim "God, you owe me!" as I shook my fist at Heaven and expected manna to fall. This is true for all of us. We become jealous and angry because we believe that God owes us and that He's failing to uphold His end of the deal.

We miss that he owes us nothing.

The only thing he owes us is His wrath over our fallen nature. Thankfully, what we get is His grace through Jesus. Completely undeserved, He has showered His goodness on us by saving us when we were yet blinded by our sin. Everything else is just icing on the cake! But to appreciate that icing, we have to understand that everything with God is a process. Maturity happens the moment we choose to believe that He is good and to trust that He will care for us—His way, in His time, with His purposes. We have to choose not to become so wrapped up in ourselves that this symptom of pride makes us crazy with our jealous thoughts. We also have to choose to change courses in thinking that God owes us, because He doesn't.

So how do we combat jealousy? Man, that's a hard one! Envy is a lot like pride in that it claims that Jesus is not enough. And, similar to pride, the best way to face off with this green-eyed monster is to slap it with some genuine humility. What does that mean? It means that you repent. Realizing that we MUST learn to be content with Jesus alone, the only response to anything besides contentment is repentance. Confessing the envy we've allowed to gain a foothold in our lives, repenting for the demands we've made because we believed that God owes us something, and praising Him for His goodness are the key steps. So do it. Now. Confess out loud those things that have burned within you. Repent for the embracing the false belief that He isn't enough. Repent for allowing pride to say that He owes you. If need be, walk away from the "kingdom" that you are so jealousy trying to protect.

Like me, you may need to lay your dream down at the altar and not pick it up again until Jesus brings it back.

What does it mean to lie something at the altar? I'll give you an example. For years, I had dreamed of owning a custom drum kit. I could imagine in my mind how amazing it would be to play the kit of my dreams, knowing that it was unlikely I'd be able to afford one any time soon...if ever. Until one day when a friend of mine decided to bless me. Offering to sell an amazing custom kit that he'd found, this man made me a ridiculously good deal that made my dreams come true. And, recognizing how excited I would be, my wife scrimped and saved to find the money we'd need to complete the deal and give me the drums I'd always wanted. The day I drove away with them, I was on cloud nine! To this day, I can still remember how thankful I was for the kindness of my friend towards a young family without much discretionary income. Now fast forward a little while. After years of fighting to make my dreams of professional drumming come true, I felt God prompting me to lay my drums on the altar. Not literally, of course. But at the same time that I felt this prompting, I also became aware of a teenage boy whose parents couldn't afford to buy him a drum set...much less one as amazing as mine. He was really passionate about drumming and would WEAR OUT the practice pad that he had, working to become better any way that he could. The day I gave him my drums, he began to cry and thank me. It opened the door for me to share Jesus and allowed me to have a relationship with him and his family from that point forward. To this day, I can hear him playing that same kit any time I'm in the neighborhood. Even better, I'm not at all ashamed to say that he's a way better drummer than I am. The day that I knew Jesus was bringing my "sacrificial gift" back to me was the moment when Letters From Patmos came about and I found myself once again blessed with an amazing drum set for practically nothing. That is the beautiful thing about allowing God to be in control. When you are willing to let go of the things you have held so tightly, it allows God to do what He will. Amazing things can begin to happen in moments like those. With that being said, I'd also like to mention that God's work in and through our lives is not in any way conditional upon our behavior or works. We don't work for His blessing, that's a false gospel. But what I want you to understand is that when you walk in obedience to the Father, you walk in His good and perfect will.

I would like to encourage you, if you're struggling with jealousy or a sense of entitlement, please lay it down. Give it to God freely and I promise that you'll be so much better off for it. The feelings of anxiety and stress that are likely haunting you now will begin to fade away the moment you declare "Jesus, this is all Yours. You owe me nothing. I give it to You, and trust that You are in control. I am choosing to believe that if You want me to have this, You will make sure that I receive it or achieve it—in Your timing."

CHAPTER SEVEN

"I was in misery, and misery is the state of every soul overcome by friendship with mortal things and lacerated when they are lost. Then the soul becomes aware of the misery which is its actual condition even before it loses them."

— *Augustine of Hippo, Confessions*

"Wait...what are you saying? What do you mean, 'you're quitting the band'?"

THESE WERE THE WORDS I said to Corey on the night he called to inform me of his decision to leave the band. We were only weeks away from signing our record deal. One of the things we'd always told each other was that if any member felt that God was telling them to step away, the rest of us would respect that with no questions asked. As a matter of fact, it had only been the year before that I had met with the guys and told them I was quitting the band and stepping out of the music industry. I had felt God telling me to step away in order to focus on Him. Note that by the time this talk with Corey occurred, I had gone through an entire year feeling the

Lord telling me that I'd gotten out of touch with Him. After I had quit, I found myself missing the travel, the joy of playing, and the friendships. I'd also still struggled with the idea of giving up on all the hard work I'd invested in the band and the progress we'd made. It seemed like such a waste. So, after about a month's absence, I asked the guys if I could come back. They hadn't found a new drummer and, to be honest, they had missed me and realized how much they relied on my business sense and drive. It had been a long month for them as well, so they were happy to welcome me back with open arms, and I was excited to be back with my brothers as we commenced pounding the pavement and playing dates.

But this conversation with Corey was different. I could hear it in his voice as we spoke, and I knew that something was different. The reality of band life is that the drummer can quit because he's replaceable. If the singer/songwriter quits... you're done for! Corey quitting was the final nail in the coffin for the rest of us band guys. Because he was my best friend, I did my best to be really honest and supportive—telling him that I also struggled with feeling burnt out, how I missed my wife and kids and wanted to be home with them. The truth was that I didn't want him to feel guilty so I was trying to give him an out. After an hour or so on the phone we hung up and that was it. We didn't talk for a couple days until I called him, hoping to convince him not to quit on all that we'd worked so hard for. We were so very close to achieving our dream that this derailing seemed unreal to me. Corey remained unwavering. He had decided to walk away and nothing that I said was changing that.

Days passed and then weeks. The other band guys and I weren't really talking. I think we all walked around in a fog, stunned at what had happened and trying to sort through our feelings. There would be no more shows, no long bus rides through the night, no gas station food, no Nashville...we were done. It had happened so abruptly that we were left in shock. There were still dates on the calendar that hadn't been played and merchandise still sitting on our bus that hadn't been sold. It felt like hitting a brick wall at 100 mph. We had so much momentum and then this one phone call brought it all to a smashing halt. It's obvious that the impact of that would hurt your physical body (if it didn't kill you!), so you can imagine that the emotional and mental side effects were similar. Personally, a small part of me was dying as I mourned the end of all that we'd worked for.

Once, when my oldest son was two years old, my wife and I decided that it would be cool for him to experience flying a kite. We drove to Walmart, purchased a cheap Elmo kite, and headed home to enjoy a fun afternoon with our little boy. I unpacked the kite and got ready to fly. (I should probably share that the parents in this story were probably more excited than our son was.) As we stood outside with the kite in hand, we noticed one crucial thing—a successful kite day requires wind and there was none! Being a dedicated dad, I refused to let my son down and decided to make my own wind. I ran across the yard full steam, looking back at my trailing kite and hoping to God that it would take off so I could be the dad of the century. At the time, we lived on a 62 acre ranch and our kite flying location was an open field. There was literally nothing but open grassland in all directions, aside from one lone telephone pole that was supported by a strong steel cable that anchored it to the ground in the midst of the vast field. Are you getting where I'm going with this story? In my haste to see my son's happiness over his airborne kite, I didn't look around as I ran. I just start running as hard as I could, looking back and yelling to my little boy, "Look, buddy! Look! Do you see the kite? Keep watching! It's going to be up in the air flying in just a minute! Just wait, ju—!" It was at that moment that the steel cable appeared out of nowhere and completely ruined my day. I hit that thing as hard as I could and was completely clotheslined by this bad boy! My feet left the ground and I hit my back. I couldn't breathe, and I was pretty sure that I was dying as I scrambled to suck in the breath that I desperately needed. And then I noticed something...my wife and son were laughing hysterically. They were laughing so hard, in fact, that my wife was actually crying and completely out of breath herself. I guess I got what I'd been looking for—a moment of laughter and joy from my son—but it hadn't been in the capacity I'd have chosen.

The jolt of having the wind knocked out of me and that moment when I found myself suddenly aware of my new surroundings as I laid on my back and tried to breathe was the same sensation that I experienced when it began to really sink in that the band was done. However, the story of our ending isn't done yet...not even close, in fact. If it had ended right here, I wouldn't have been so distraught over the way things played out. I would've slowly adjusted to my new reality and life would've moved on. More importantly, I wouldn't have any reason to be writing this story.

A couple weeks passed and I decided that I had to do something with myself. I had a family depending on me to provide for their care, and the more time that I spent sitting around, thinking about the band, the more depressed I was becoming. A friend found me a job working as a valet at a local hospital and I began work there. Dustin, the now ex-guitar player, was looking for work too, so I recommended him and we both were thankful for the opportunity to make some money. It definitely didn't pay huge stacks of cash, but I felt satisfaction in the fact that—for the first time in a while—I was bringing home money and paying the bills. I was beginning to adjust.

One night after work, I received a phone call from Corey. We hadn't talked since he'd made his decision to leave the band, so I was excited to hear from him. The silence we'd experienced the last couple weeks wasn't due to hurt feelings or anger. I think he'd been giving me space to adjust to my new band-free life, and I was thankful to have it. Regardless, the shock was wearing off and I was happy to talk to him. I'll even admit that, before I answered, thoughts began pouring through my mind as to why he was calling. Had he changed his mind? Did he regret quitting? Was the band going to pick up where we'd left off? It was impossible not to entertain a little hope that the shock I'd experienced wasn't really going to last and that things could go back to what they'd been. I picked up the phone and engaged in a little chitchat before Corey hit me with a question that caught me as odd. He wanted to know who owned the name of the band and how many CDs we had left to sell. Unsure why he'd be asking, I probed a little bit and was completely unprepared for the response he gave.

"I've decided to sign as a writer and solo artist..."

So after two years of traveling together and only weeks away from signing our record deal together, he decides to sign our deal without us? What is going on here?

I don't really remember anything he said after that because I was stunned. Do you remember me mentioning that I don't handle some things well? In chapter three, I talked about how I struggle with being questioned and having people go against what I decide. Well, I can add another to that list because I didn't handle this well either. I don't handle betrayal well and that is exactly what this felt like to me.

Some of you may be thinking, *I would have been upset too! You had every right to be mad!* And I would agree. Here's the problem. If I had only thought about some of the reasons why he'd want to be solo (ahem...do you recall my blow up in Ohio?) and had remained calm enough to talk this over with him, a friendship may have been salvaged. But I didn't. Yet again, my knee jerk reactions took over and I was instantly irate. I accused him of having planned this all along, of having used the rest of us to attain notice in Nashville and then just leaving us in the dirt while he continued to ascend alone. After that, I hung up the phone, aching over the anger and hurt that I was experiencing and feeling completely betrayed.

Have you ever heard the sayings, "when it rains it pours," or maybe, "today is just not my day"? I've always thought those cliche sayings were completely overdramatic, but they seemed to fit the moment. In fact, it seemed that it just wasn't my month—or my year! It wasn't just raining, there was a tsunami flood and I couldn't seem to keep my head above water as the waves crashed over me.

The next wave hit a few days after my phone call from Corey. My wife and I were at a dinner party that Dustin and his wife were attending as well. We were having a great time with our friends, laughing and enjoying being in each other's company. I could tell that Dustin wanted to tell me something, but it wasn't the time or place. I asked Dustin if he'd had the opportunity to play guitar lately and he shared that he had a little and then mentioned that we needed to talk later. When we had a moment to slip away, we stepped outside and he proceeded to drop a bomb on me as gently as he could. Corey had decided to play the remaining shows by himself and had asked the rest of the band to play for him. He wasn't planning on asking me.

There it was.

This was the thing that would completely break me. This was the moment that the enemy would use to destroy my spirit and make me want to turn my back on everything I held dear—my family, my friends, my church and my God. I was already struggling with the feeling of having been betrayed by my friend, so finding out that the band I had worked hard to build was going to continue to play without me hurt more than I could handle. It's sort of like being the last kid picked on the playground...except I hadn't been picked at all. My friends had chosen to exclude me and the rejection I felt was acute. Not only had my dreams gone up in smoke, but now I felt betrayed by the entire group of guys that I had once looked to as brothers. To this day, I will never be able to express the gratitude that I felt for Dustin's friendship throughout this time. He truly was, and continues to be, a man of integrity that I hope to emulate. The night he broke the news to me, he didn't come with the intent of instigating drama. Dustin is a peaceful man and he spoke to me as a friend who was trying to soften what he knew would be a painful blow to my ego.

I want to clearly say that I'm not telling you this story to make Corey out to be the bad guy, because I'm telling you that he's not. Is he perfect? No. He would tell you, himself, that he didn't handle things well throughout this ordeal either. I know now, looking back on it, why he didn't ask me. I can be pretty hostile! Don't get me wrong, I don't go around looking for a fight and if you know me at all you would know that I try hard to be patient, kind and Jesus-like. But, like anyone who is trying to handle the stresses of life, family and finances, I have a tendency to be human and fall back into my own sinful hang-ups. The night in Ohio that I mention in Chapter 3 where I completely lose my head and tear Corey down with my words, is a great example of my humanity at it's worst. I'd been raised to be a fighter and that rough-around-the-edges kid inside me was begging Corey to get up and fight me. Yelling profanities, wishing he would react so that I could release my frustration on his jawline was a clear sign that I'd left behind my Christ model. So I'll ask you—if you had to deal with a person who you'd had an experience like that with, would you want to be the one who breaks bad news to them? Even more, would you want to commit yourself to being in close quarters for two months while you travel in a cramped bus and lead people in worship to Jesus of all things? Yeah, I can't say that I would either.

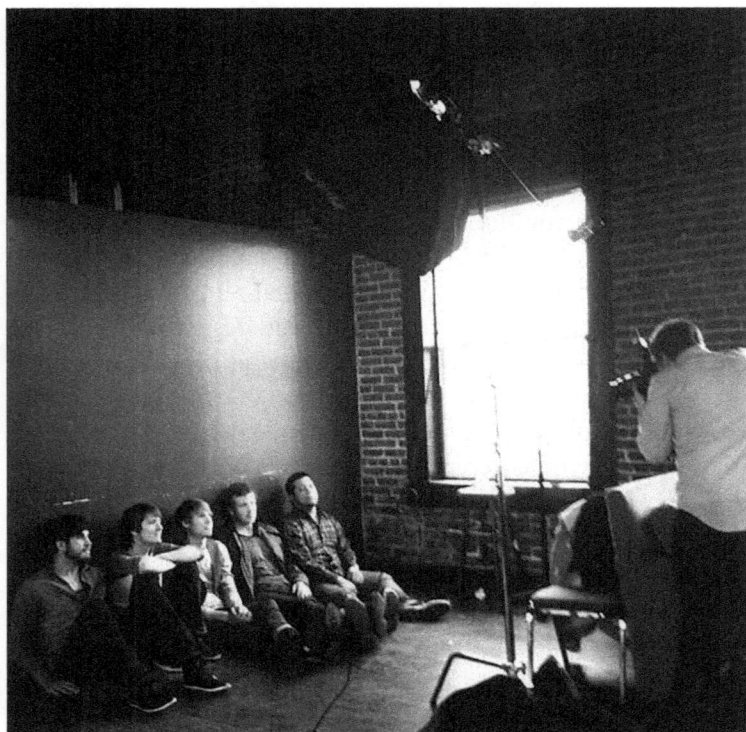

Photo Shoot

CHAPTER EIGHT

"An idol is anything we trust in for deliverance in the place of Jesus and his grace."

—*Scotty Smith*

WHEN DUSTIN TOLD ME ABOUT Corey's plans to find someone else to play drums, I felt something in my heart change. Deep down inside, the flesh part of me that I tried hard to suppress was rising to the surface. The ugly things that we humans do our best to keep hidden from polite society were beginning to come out and who I am without Jesus made a roaring appearance!

I rushed my wife into the car and began the drive to pick up our kids from a friend's house. I can remember doing 90 mph down a county road, screaming at the top of my lungs and cussing the heavens. I alternated between flipping God off and punching the steering wheel as the hurt I felt inside manifested in a boiling rage. My coping method is obviously anger. When I am really hurting, it's easier for me to be angry than it is to cry it out, so that is what I turn to in the worst circumstances. I felt as if everyone in my life had betrayed me (other than my wife and kids, of course)…my manager, the label, my band mates, and the God that I had claimed loved me. The more I screamed my frustrations, the more angry I became and the more my heart seemed to turn to cement. With every punch and explicative, I wasn't relieving anger—I was fueling it! Then words I thought I would NEVER say erupted from my mouth *"God is NOT real and IF he is, he's definitely NOT good!"*

I confess that hearing those words coming out of my own mouth even rattled me a bit. I don't even want to think what my poor wife was enduring as she sat in silence through the torrent. I had thought that speaking the ugly thoughts rushing through my spirit would be therapeutic. Instead, I felt an even stronger rush of anger, bitterness, and hatred filling me. We arrived at our friends' house and I stood outside while Traci went in and got the kids ready to leave. She must have explained a little of what was going on because my dear friend (and pastor) came out and stood with me for a few moments. I could sense that he wanted to say something to help, but in the face of the anger that was emanating from me, even he was left speechless. And this is a man who provides spiritual coaching for a living! You know it's bad when a counselor has no counsel for you. Once I'd calmed down enough to be somewhat civil, I came in and gathered my family, briefly thanked our friends for babysitting, and headed home at a legal speed.

As days passed, bitterness began to poison my soul. My hatred for everyone that had anything to do with my time in the band was all that I could think about. I spent the next week distancing myself from any and all connections to Letters From Patmos. If you were friends with me on Facebook and I only knew you because of my correlation with the band, I blocked you. If you called about the band, I ignored your phone call. It's like I wanted to take the piece of my brain that stored those memories and cut it out. You might be thinking that I'm being crazy and overly dramatic about this entire ordeal and you may be right, but when you come face to face with the realization that your faith has been in the wrong place, it hurts. The idol that I'd hoped would bring my salvation—fame, fortune, validation of all my hard work, and the life I'd dreamed of—had completely shattered before my very eyes and I'd been left without a foundation to fall back on. Unknowingly, I had removed Jesus from the throne of my heart and had relegated him to the role of a handy catchphrase that I used to cover my idolatry. This moment is what I referenced at the beginning of the book. I share it because I want to drive home this truth—**it is easier to release an idol from an open palm.** My hands had been holding this idol with a white knuckled grasp for so long, that when God crushed my idol it left me reeling from the pain.

During my week of selfishness and hatred, I had decided that I was becoming an atheist. I didn't pray or read my Bible and I refused to go to church. My wife, in God-given wisdom, left me to my own devices and gave me the freedom to work out my own salvation. I know for a fact that she was faithfully praying for me and had placed me in the safest place she could—God's hands. We'd been married about eight years at this point, so she'd had plenty of experience when it came to dealing with me. Normally, she'd confront me about my selfish behavior and challenge me to be the godly man that I'm called to be. While I usually get annoyed at first, I have to confess that I love that about her because I know that I can always trust her counsel and discernment. This week I believe that she sensed there was something different about what I was feeling because she never once mentioned how awful I has behaving. She quietly offered me her love and support... until she sensed that it was time for change. The night arrived when she confronted me and told me that it was time to move on. When I got angry, she calmly informed me that I could sleep on the couch and keep my bad attitude to myself until I was once again ready to be the man she had married. That night on the couch, I was awakened by the voice of

God. Now, before you start asking questions, this was not an audible voice. However, it was VERY clear in my spirit that the God of the universe wanted my attention. The message was stern and clear, and I know that it was Him because I was completely uninterested in hearing from Him, so I had no reason to fabricate it. I wasn't looking for guidance or help, and I no longer cared about my dreams or calling. As far as I was concerned, that was all garbage and I was moving on with my life without God. So trust me when I say, I heard Him. He said to me, "*I've shown you mercy*". This was not at all what I wanted to hear and, to be honest, I was completely aggravated that He would dare to say such a thing after all that He had just allowed to happen to me. I sat straight up on the couch and said out loud, **"Shown me mercy? How have you shown me mercy? I've lost everything! Friends, money, my dreams...and I'm not any better off after having wasted two and half years of my life in that stupid band for YOU!"**

Quick pause, are you familiar with that moment in the Bible when Job is yelling at God and asking why He has allowed all the tragedy in his life? He then goes on to accuse God of allowing a lot of junk and injustice in life in general. Job says something along the lines of "Hey! I was living right. I wasn't sinning. I took care of my family. In case you've missed it, I've upheld my end of the bargain here! God, you suck because you're totally slacking on your end!" Do you remember how God responds then? He asks Jobs some question that would highlight just how small Job (and mankind) is. The Creator of the universe begins by warning Job that he will need to "brace himself like a man" before this conversation goes any further. In some translations, the text says "dress for action like a man" which sounds a bit like a warrior getting his gear on. It's obvious that God means business about whatever He's about to say. Once the warning is issued, God then begins to ask him things like:

- **Where were you when I laid the foundation of the earth?**

- **Or, who shut in the sea with doors?**

- **Have you commanded the morning since your days began and caused it to know its place...? (Job 38 ESV)**

My late night couch episode was a "Job moment," if you will. After responding to God with such defiance and arrogance, He proceeded to tell me the many ways that He's shown me mercy.

"The fact that I let you take your next breath after blaspheming my name is me showing you mercy."

And just like that, I was speechless. Immediately humbled and brought low. I realized with crystal-like clarity what I had been doing for years. Making the band my proverbial "golden calf"—the idol in my life—I had done what'd I'd mocked the Israelites for doing in Exodus 32. I had taken God from His rightful place in my life and heart, placing the band, fame, success, and money on His throne. I also realized, for probably the first time ever, what a skewed view of the Father I had. Unknowingly, I had looked to Him as a great big vending machine in the sky that simply required the right actions to unlock His blessings. If I could just learn what buttons to push, He'd rain down goodness on my life. If I would fast, read certain books, pray just the right words and kneel just the right way... in other words, if I would dance like a monkey and perform well, then God would accept me and give me what my heart desired. After all, Psalm 37:4 says, "*delight in the Lord and he will give you the desires of your heart.*" Wasn't that what I was doing when I was "performing" or doing my Christian duties? Wasn't I delighting in him by *doing* these things? The answer is,

65

NO. The sad truth about our Western culture is that we've got God so wrong. For some reason, we think that by doing "right" things we can attract and entice God to love us and bless us. I'd been in ministry as a youth pastor for four years prior to being in the band, so you would think I would have understood this. I preached it, so surely I knew it! But, I didn't. And the truth is, I don't think the majority of people do.

In order to keep our hearts from idolatry, we must understand that God never asks us to earn His love. We already have it! And this is key. In fact, it's one of the very foundations of our belief system. Without grasping this, it is impossible to mature in our relationship with the Father. Without understanding His great love, we will always find ourselves acting like orphans stealing bread from the table, because we don't understand that we've been made part of the family and are welcome to the feast. You have a place at the table! Don't steal it. You can't earn it. It's just yours for the taking because of what Christ has done for you. No longer orphans, we are called to live as children of a loving Father who gladly takes care of us.

Several years ago, my wife and I were foster parents at a group home for kids who were unable to be placed in "regular" foster homes for various mental, emotional, or behavioral reasons. We lived in a cottage with 8-10 teenage boys (ages 12-17 years old) and acted as their parents. Many of them had been abused in one capacity or another. Regardless of abuse, almost all of them had been neglected either intentionally or because their parents were unable to care for them properly. It was during our time there that I experienced what an "orphan heart" truly looks like.

Every night for dinner we would sit down at a huge dining room table and share a meal. Because these were teenage boys, I'm sure you understand that it took a LOT of food to feed the kids at that table! My wife and I would have platters of fried chicken, mashed potatoes, green beans, corn, and dinner rolls with dessert waiting in the wings. Every boy ate until they were full. After the meal, we'd spend time together playing games watching movies or talking and then it'd be time for bed. Well, late one night, Traci and I heard a noise in the kitchen. I got out of bed and went to check it out. There stood a couple of our boys, raiding the fridge! Upon further investigation, we discovered leftover food hidden in drawers in their rooms. Gross, right? Yes, it was. At first, we were shocked—why would they hide food? Don't they know how sick old food can make them? What would possess them? And then we realized. Thanks to some of the traumas of their pasts, these kids lived with an inner fear that the food wouldn't always be available to them. As I said, some had experienced abuse (food being withheld as a form of punishment) and some had come from neglect (Mom can't buy groceries when she's too high to function and all the money goes to drugs). Although they had been living in a safe place for YEARS, the fear was still so deeply engrained in them that they lived in reaction to it.

When we don't grasp God's love for us and when we believe that His love is conditional upon our actions or performances, then we act just like my foster boys. Unable to understand that we have a good Father who will never withhold any good thing (according to His wisdom), we find ourselves grasping desperately at bread and missing the feast. The good things in our lives become idols because we don't trust His goodness and feel that we must secure our own blessings at whatever cost. The beauty of knowing that your Father has your best interest in mind and that He loves you unconditionally is that you can live a life of peace and freedom rather than snacking on moldy bread in the dark.

The other realization that I had that night on the couch was that, even if I spent the rest of my life in poverty and loneliness, the work Christ did on the cross was ENOUGH. He is ALL that I need and everything else is simply icing on the cake. In light of that, it was a lot easier to see that God truly had shown me mercy. This made His words to be much less bitter to swallow and much more joyous.

When God began His restoring work in me that night, I began to devour scripture like I had never done before. Guys like Matt Chandler, John Piper and Tim Keller were on my podcast playlist, and I kept their sermons going nonstop. I began to study suffering and contentment and soon found myself in the book of Philippians. In fact, that book is one of my favorites of the New Testament to this day. In Philippians, Paul is writing a letter to the church at Philippi while he is imprisoned in Rome. He is chained to a guard in a dank cell, waiting to find out if he will be put to death or not, when he writes this, *"Indeed, I count everything as loss because of the surpassing worth of knowing Christ Jesus my Lord. For his sake I have suffered the loss of all things and count them as rubbish in order that I may gain Christ." (3:8 ESV)*

So let me conclude this chapter with the following truths. There is nothing else that is more important, beautiful or life-giving than the love of Jesus Christ. When we recognize that Paul was right when he said that everything in this world is garbage compared to the mystery of salvation, we are grasping that which is the most valuable. If you never memorize the entire Bible, pray for ten hours straight, or do any other form of extreme spiritual disciplines, know that the one thing that you must do is to focus your life and prize on Jesus and let everything else fall to the wayside.

CHAPTER NINE

You are never too old to set another goal or to dream a new dream.

—C.S. Lewis

NOW TO THE CHAPTER THAT I have been looking forward to writing - and the one I hope you've been looking forward to reading! This chapter is all about dreams. And no, I'm not talking about the kind that happen while you're drooling on your pillow each night. The dreams I'm referring to are the things that you daydream about. They are the longings in your heart for the future and the good things that you hope will come about. They are the things you feel that you were created to do and the passions that reside deep within your being.

Some people have simple dreams. They revolve around growing up, getting married, raising children and providing for their family with a career that they enjoy. Their goals in life mainly center on being faithful, cultivating a family that loves the Lord, and enjoying their grandkids in the latter years of life. Those are good dreams. These types of dreams are stable, encourage healthy foundations and godly living—making them a good thing and pleasing to the Lord. Hear me when I say that I'm not demeaning those dreams in this chapter. But I'm also not talking about those dreams.

There are other dreams in life that are different from these foundational ones. They are dreams like becoming a professional athlete, a politician, or a musician. They consist of a desire to be known, to achieve greatness and to reach one's fullest potential. The result of these dreams is often fame and fortune. My dream of the music world fits into this category.

As a kid (and before I learned to play drums), I dreamed of becoming a professional baseball player. I dominated little league like a boss and then went to high school and realized that it just wasn't for me. Everyone had grown up and become faster, stronger, and bigger...which meant that I had to work harder to stay on top of my game. I wasn't interested in that, so I learned to play drums and changed my dream to professional musicianship. With dreams like this, the common themes are fame, money, power and prestige. Those are great advantages IF you have the character and integrity to back them. Maybe you've witnessed what happens when someone's character isn't in line with their gifts. They accomplish their dreams only to crash and burn a short while later because they couldn't handle the responsibility of all they were given. Case in point, my story.

To help you avoid this fall back to earth experience and to accomplish great things with you, God will often take you through a process of refining. I would liken it to an experience in the military in which you are trained to be a person worthy of being called a soldier. They send you to boot camp to teach you how to manage your fears, handle yourself well in the worse situations, and live up to your title overall. God will do the same thing as He molds you into the person that you need to be in order to do great things through Him. For some, this process is a short season of life. For others, especially those with a particularly unique calling, it will be a lifetime of learning. A great biblical example of this is Joseph the dreamer. We find his story in the book of Genesis.

At around the age of 12, Joseph has a dream from God in which he sees stars bowing down to another star. He then has the same dream with wheat bowing down to another sheath of wheat. The lead star/wheat bundle being honored in his dreams was, of course, Joseph himself. The other stars/wheat bundles represented his father and brothers. Now, do you remember what I just said about going through a process in life? This is where we find the beginning of Joseph's process. If you are reading this book and you are an older sibling, you can probably easily admit that the idea of kowtowing to a younger sibling has never been part of your plan in life. In case younger siblings aren't annoying enough, the idea of bowing down to one is pretty insulting. Joseph, like most kid brothers, just couldn't wait to tell his family about his dream. Big mistake. Finding his brothers at work in a field, he pridefully begins to share this vivid dream that he'd had. When I read this portion of the story, I can almost imagine exactly how that must have gone down. Joseph walks up wearing the flashy new coat that their dad had given him. The coat was proof that he was dad's favorite, so wearing it was like rubbing salt into a wound. As they sweat and toiled in the field, up saunters Joseph as he starts to chat. "Hey jerks! Remember that beating you gave me last week?" (I'm sure they all laughed and high-fived each other at this reminder) "Well, first off, I want all you smelly ogres to take a close look at what I'm wearing. Dad gave me this to show everyone that I'm his favorite. How's that feel? And the other thing I want you to know is that I had this awesome dream that I think was from God. It told me that you are going to bow down to me one day! And you know what? When that day comes, I'll remember every wedgie, every punch in the arm, and every booger you made me eat growing up. And I'll especially remember the beating you gave me the other day and you will ALL PAY!" It was probably around this point that they decided to grab him and pummel him before he could run his mouth more and then run back to Daddy, per the style of a younger sibling. After roughing him up, they decided to rid themselves of their pesky problem once and for all. Throwing him in a pit as they found some slave traders, Joseph's brothers likely felt like they were going to come out ahead in this plan. Their bratty kid brother would be gone and their pockets would be a little heavier, thanks to his sale into slavery.

Let's move forward in the story. Joseph is sold by his brothers and turns up in Egypt where a man name Potiphar purchases him. Joseph does well in Potiphar's house and earns the praise of his master. Unfortunately, he also earns the attention of Potiphar's wife. She happens to be extremely interested in the good-looking cabana boy and decides to take advantage of his position. She tries to come on to Joseph, but God has already done enough work in his character that he very humbly and respectfully declines her lustful invitations. Let's pause for a second and appreciate that. Here we have Joseph, who was likely around 17 years old and full of hormones, turning down the advances of an older woman. That's pretty impressive when you consider the fact that David committed adultery and had the woman's husband killed, yet was still considered a man after God's heart! Despite his many good attributes, David obviously struggled with (and lost) in his fight against temptation. The only thing I can figure about Joseph is that God had obviously been doing a great work to prepare him for this moment of testing.

After Joseph declines her offer, Mrs. Potiphar does not handle his rejection well. Outraged, she makes up a story about how Joseph assaulted her and has him thrown in jail and left to rot. Hell hath no fury like a spurned woman? Again, I have to point back to the work God is doing in Joseph. Despite the sad state of his affairs, Joseph is still clinging to the promise of God's goodness and his belief that God would use him one day to do something great. If I were Joseph, I would have been thinking that God was either lying or that I just ate too much pizza the night before those dreams because it is definitely not looking like He's elevating me to any special position right about now.

While in jail, Joseph makes some friends and reveals that he has a knack for interpreting dreams. Let's fast forward some now and you'll see that this gift for dream interpretation earns him a get out of jail free card when Joseph is given the opportunity to interpret a particularly puzzling dream that Pharaoh has been losing sleep over. In the dream, Pharaoh is being warned about an upcoming famine. After interpreting, Joseph is also able to instruct Pharaoh on what to do to get through these hard times. In turn, Pharaoh makes him the second in command over all of Egypt. Talk about a rags to riches story! As the famine ravages the land, who do you think should come straggling in looking for provisions? You got it—Joseph's long lost brothers! Except they don't know that it's him. The kid they tossed in a ditch has become a powerful and capable man. They bow down to this leader of Egypt—just like in the dream—and Joseph accepts them with humility and grace. I'm skipping a lot of the details in the end of this story and taking liberties in the telling of it, but hopefully you're getting my drift, right? God made Joseph for a purpose. And God made you for a purpose as well. We know this because Jeremiah chapter 1 says it pretty clearly as God speaks to Jeremiah,

> *"Before I formed you in the womb I knew you, and before you were born I consecrated you; I appointed you a prophet to the nations."*

Before the foundation of the Earth, God knew us by name and gave us a purpose. Our purpose is meant to bring fulfillment to our lives and glory to His name. However, before we can live in this purpose, we are just like Joseph. There is a process we must go through, and this process helps us to be more capable of handling the responsibility that living a dream will bring.

You may be asking yourself, how do I know what my dream is? How do I know if it's from God or not? Those are great questions! There are a few questions that you can ask yourself or take some time to meditate on.

- What do you love to do? In my life, I've found that I love reading/studying/teaching Scripture and I love playing music. Both of these are parts of who God created me to be and they make me unique. The thought of getting to do either of these things makes me glad. As a friend of mine says, it "gets the happy bubbles in my head going!" So, what makes your happy bubbles go?

- What am I good at? As I pointed out earlier, I loved baseball as a kid. But as others began to excel, I discovered that I wasn't in love with it enough to give the effort it took to keep from plateauing. It's similar to wanting to play pro football, but being unable to surpass 125 lbs on the scales. You have to realistically be good enough to accomplish a dream and then have the drive to do so. Both of those are important. Some people are very naturally gifted, but have no drive to accomplish any goals. That was true of me and baseball. Others have a lot of drive, but just don't have the ability to accomplish their goal because it's not what God created them to do. A good indication as to whether or not you have what it takes to do something is that you enjoy the challenge it provides and that others notice how well you perform at it. And by others, I mean more people than your family or the friends you have who are too nice to "burst your bubble" and tell the truth. So what is it? What is the thing that you love to do and that you are better than the average Joe at doing?

- Does it bring glory to God? This is the final and most important question on the list and it CANNOT be overlooked! Does what you dream of doing honor God? What I mean by that is this—your dream should promote God's glory. For example, you could be in love with drugs and be really good at selling them...but we both know that there's no God-glory or honor found there. A God dream should bring life to others, not destroy it. Another good example is dancing. You may be an amazing dancer, but if that leads to seductive moves and skimpy clothes (or stripping them off all the way), your dream is not in its proper place. Are you catching what I'm throwing here? I'm not trying to say that you have to want to be a pastor or missionary or something like that, but what I am saying is that whatever you dream of has to be legal and it has to bring honor to the Creator. It's also good to remember that your gifting is not just intended to be for you. We are gifted so that others can be blessed. We are called to build up and encourage others. In my case, I used my gifting as a musician for selfish purposes. What had been given to me as a means of ushering others into worship later became a tool that I used to build my own platform of fame. This is why we must remember that our gifts are not for us, they're for our neighbors. If you and I can remember that truth, it will keep us humble and focused on Christ. And humility will keep us from creating idols out of our dreams.

God has destined you for a purpose. I want you to totally understand this. There is greatness inside every one of His children. Not one child of His was created without a special purpose and gifting. However, in order to walk in that gifting, each one of us must learn that it's all about cultivating the character and understanding required to be on the receiving end of all the glory that a great purpose can bring.

One last thing that I'd like to point out before I wrap up this chapter is that there is an exception to the "what are you good at?" rule. I have to confess that God will sometimes use things that we don't feel that we're good at in order to get the glory. For me, writing this book is a great example. I never in a million years would've thought that I'd write a book. Until I met my lovely and intelligent wife, I had actually gone through life believing that I wasn't the academic type and that books were better as shelf decorations. She challenged me to begin reading as a means of growing spiritually and— surprise!—I soon discovered that I am an avid reader. Of course, that didn't immediately translate into a desire to write books...but at least I actually appreciated them for the first time! Writing doesn't come naturally to me. BUT I know that God uses that fact as a means of keeping me dependent upon Him. Without seeking Him with all I am to formulate the words of these chapters, it's highly likely that I'd produce pages of rambling nothingness that nobody wants to read. Keep that in mind if you think that your dream in life may look a certain way, only to discover that God mixes things up on you. Be open to allowing Him to cultivate new dreams inside you as He reveals hidden talents that even you aren't aware of yet. The seasons of preparation that you walk through will often reveal gems of self-revelation as He reveals aspects of your giftings or personality that you may not have ever known existed.

Just like Joseph, we must all remember to cling to the promise of God. Knowing that He will accomplish His good work in our lives in the perfect time, we can trust Him. Remember to be on the look out for symptoms of idolatry as you walk through the process of life. If you find yourself becoming obsessed, prideful or jealous of others, it's time to take a step back and spend time with your loving Father. Know that I'm cheering for you and that I want to see you achieve the things that God is revealing for your future! If you haven't discovered those things yet, know that I'm praying that God will begin to reveal them.

The Whole Letters Family

Photo credit:Chris Pochiba

At Oral Roberts University

Photo Credit: Will Knowles

CHAPTER TEN

I WANT TO LEAVE YOU with a glimpse into what God has done with the lives of each member of the band since the time we broke up until now. Before I do that, I want to tell you that God has healed my heart as well as redeeming my friendships with each of my ex-band mates. So know this: when God allows darkness and valleys to shatter your reality, He already has a plan for redemption! He knows what will bring Him glory and what will ultimately be best for all involved. It's awesome to know that I serve a God who is all knowing and all-powerful! Nothing can happen without Him allowing it, which tells me that He has every situation under control!

After a long period of not speaking, Corey (the lead singer) and I gradually began getting reacquainted as we made the long walk towards forgiveness. If you've ever had a chance to forgive someone that you feel has betrayed you and left you deeply hurting, you know that this is not an overnight process. It takes a great deal of prayer, as well as time, to heal the wound. The good news is that, no matter how deep the wound, we serve a God who is in the healing business, as long as we are willing to let Him do it. The moment that marked a corner turning for me occurred on the day I learned to pray for Corey. I don't mean generic prayers, but specific things. I would feel the Holy Spirit impressing on me the need to pray for his success in the music industry and that he would write songs that would bring freshness to the worship of the church. Remember in chapter 5 when I talked about humility and Jesus washing the feet of the disciples, even though they would betray Him and deny Him? These prayers were my way of "washing feet" as I swallowed my pride and allowed God to use me as an intercessor for blessing in Corey's life. I still do this pretty much every week by praying for him, or by sending him a quick text message to encourage him and to share my appreciation for his gifting and for the place God now has him. I can also tell you that, from my perspective nowadays, it makes me smile to know that God used me in a small way to help Corey get to Nashville and write songs that will impact the church body worldwide. I love seeing how God works not only in our lives but in the lives of others—even when we are failing!

So what is Corey up to now? Well, he did sign that song writing deal and works with Centric Worship. He's had the opportunity to partner with other writers and create some pretty amazing songs that I know he's excited about sharing with the body of Christ. Personally, I'm excited too! I can still remember that night at Southeastern University when we stood in amazement as the crowd sang the lyrics to our song "Coming to Save Us." I was so proud then and I know I will be proud again when I'm able to witness the church singing out the new words God has given my friend. If you're interested in hearing what songs are out now, I'd encourage you to check out Corey Voss Music. I know that the songs the Holy Spirit has given him will be a blessing to you.

My faithful friend, Dustin (the guitar player), just welcomed his first child into the world. He and his sweet wife Haley are now the proud parents of a handsome baby boy! My wife and

I could not be more excited for them or surer that their son is blessed with the very best parents. Dustin continues to be the man of integrity that he has been all along, and I continue to be blessed with his friendship. I look forward to watching his son grow up to be a true man of God, like his father. I pray that my own sons are blessed with friends like Dustin in their lives. When the band ended, Dustin started a company for guitar players and gear heads called GearWire. If you're a guitar player who loves smoking guitar licks and talking shop, do yourself a favor and go check out gearwire.com. You'll be glad you did, I assure you.

Ralph (the bass guitar player) and his lovely wife, Holly, moved back to his hometown of Houston, Texas where they are both working hard and waiting on God's next move in their lives. Ralph is feeling the call to music ministry and continues to play bass guitar whenever he has the chance, as he waits on God's timing.

Ben (the other guitar player) loves to spend his days working out and flexing! One day very soon he will have the biggest biceps in the music industry to go along with his killer guitar chops. He will soon graduate from college with a degree in accounting and has been blessed to be able to travel, playing guitar as a "hired gun" for a southern gospel group.

Josh, our babysitter and sound engineer, lives in the same state that I now reside in—Arkansas. Sadly, we don't live in the same town, but with a little gas money we can make a weekend visit happen. He works at a local pharmacy by day, but is still showing off his technical prowess weekly through various opportunities that arise to run sound for churches or companies in need of his services. He recently had the opportunity to run sound for a large event featuring America's favorite family—the Robertson's from the hit television show Duck Dynasty on A&E!

As for me, God has blessed me tremendously! After what felt like months of hell, God led me through the journey of healing and restoration that I mention throughout this book. Once I'd found my foundation again, He brought me to my true calling. You see, for years I had assumed that my ultimate dream was to play music and to travel the world. Through my time of restoration, I began to realize that the life I love most is preaching the Word, discipling, and being able to spend time loving my wife and raising my kids. When a door opened to become a student pastor in Arkansas, I took it and moved my family to begin a new adventure. It's been here, in a small town hidden in the mountains of Arkansas, that I've realized I'm called to minister to the church of the future by discipling the youth of today. God has given me a burden to see this generation of young people do great things for Him—to confront the darkness they find in this world and to bring Light. Challenging them to believe that they are capable of doing big things for Jesus (as long as they keep Him first!) was also what propelled me to write this book. This new sense of call allowed me to realize that my dream is to write, preach, and disciple young people. I want to encourage them to seek out their God-given dreams and to walk with integrity as they are used by God to change the world. Being off the road and home has been a huge blessing as well. My wife and I are enjoying life with our beautiful children, raising them to be world changers who do great things through God-given dreams. It puts a never-ending smile on my face to know that I get to come home each day to a houseful of laughter, sword fights, tea parties, and diaper changing duty, rather than having to live through phone calls and pictures texted to my phone. I also prefer crawling into bed each night with my best friend—my beautiful wife—as we laugh over inside jokes or the silly antics of our kids, rather than climbing into a bunk bed with five smelly guys snacking on gas station food.

God knows what He's doing when He takes you through the things He does. I'm still learning not to fight the path God has me on and to just let Him do what He does, because what

He's doing is making me more like Him. I get better at it every time I consider His faithfulness and love towards me. We are the clay that Isaiah refers to when he says that God is the potter. He's working us and shaping us so that when it's all finished and He's refined us and held us up to the flame, He can take a step back and see His Son! Don't fight those moments of discipline or valley. Know they are gifts from God, even when it may not seem like it at first. When all is said and done, you'll be on the other side of that trial, and I promise that you'll see that it was worth it...even if it was hard. I know that I wouldn't trade my "valley" time for anything in the world. If I had it to do over again, I would definitely want to do things differently (don't we all wish we could go back and do things better?), but I would never trade the adventures I had and the lessons I learned. It was each of those experiences that made me who I am as a believer in Christ. It was my failing that taught me that my identity is not in a band or even as a musician. I learned that my identity was not in being a husband, father or a pastor. My identity is rooted in the One who makes me whole and who has redeemed my soul, Jesus Christ.

So now that you know what's going on in our lives, let me leave you with one last challenge. If you've found yourself in a place of valleys or heartache, take a step back. Cling to Him with everything you have and focus on Jesus. Then, when the time is right, chase your dream and see it through. Give all you have to Jesus and see what He does through you! You were made to be great. You were made to do things that only you can do at this time, in this very hour. Love Jesus with all that you are, wait patiently for Him and watch the greatness that God is!

ABOUT THE AUTHOR

LOGAN MERRICK IS A STUDENT PASTOR at First Baptist Church in Mena, Arkansas. He believes that the youth of today are the church of tomorrow and is committed to pastoring young people and raising up a generation of world changers. Logan and his wife Traci have four beautiful children and enjoy living life together as they write, minister, and raise their kids to love Jesus.

www.ingramcontent.com/pod-product-compliance
Lightning Source LLC
Chambersburg PA
CBHW030850090426
42737CB00009B/1178